Gardeners'
Worldmagazine

101 Ideas for Veg
from Small Spaces

10 9 8 7 6 5 4 3 2 1
Published in 2009 by BBC Books,
an imprint of Ebury Publishing
A Random House Group Company

Copyright © Woodlands Books Limited 2009
Words by Jane Moore
All photographs © *Gardeners' World Magazine*

The Random House Group Limited Reg. No. 954009

Addresses for companies within the Random House Group can be
found at www.randomhouse.co.uk

A CIP catalogue record for this book is available from the British Library.

ISBN 9781846077326

The Random House Group Limited supports The Forest Stewardship
Council (FSC), the leading international forest certification organization.
All our titles that are printed on Greenpeace approved FSC certified
paper carry the FSC logo. Our paper procurement policy can be found
at www.rbooks.co.uk/environment

Commissioning editor: Lorna Russell
Project editor: Helena Caldon
Designer: Kathryn Gammon
Picture researcher: Janet Johnson
Production controller: Lucy Harrison

Colour origination by Dot Gradations Ltd
Printed and bound in Germany by Firmengruppe APPL,
aprinta druck, Wemding

Gardeners'
Worldmagazine

101 Ideas for Veg from Small Spaces
DELICIOUS CROPS FROM TINY PLOTS

Author
Jane Moore

BOOKS

Contents

6

Introduction

There's no doubt that growing your own fruit and vegetables is hugely satisfying, even if you only have a tiny space in which to garden. Cleverly managed, the smallest space can produce a wealth of delicious, home-grown crops that are bound to be fresher and tastier than anything on offer in the shops.

Many vegetables are surprisingly fast growing and will tolerate the most awkward and unpromising corners, providing fresh flavoursome food that's ready to harvest in no time at all. Whether you have a garden, a balcony or even a window box, you can still grow a wide range of vegetables and enjoy harvesting your own produce whenever you want.

Small spaces are often just as productive as larger ones if you grow a succession of crops – replacing harvested crops with new plants within days – and if you make the most of walls and fences, raised beds and unusual containers. This book will help you maximise the potential of every available nook and cranny. With *101 Ideas for Veg from Small Spaces* to guide you, not only will your crops taste good, but your garden will look good too!

Whether you're new to gardening or an old hand at growing your own, these ideas will give you the inspiration to make the most of even the smallest space.

Jane Moore
Gardeners' World Magazine

Beautiful baby beetroots

Fast-growing beetroots look and taste lovely and they make a really useful quick crop among longer-term veg.

Time to sow: Spring through to late summer. Plant out seedlings in modules once well rooted.

Beetroots come in a wide range of shapes and colours – not just the usual red globes. Varieties with golden or striped roots are particularly attractive, but there are also tapered varieties and even a pure white form, which is useful as it won't stain your clothes when you chop it up.

Start sowing in spring under cloches and keep going until mid-summer, as baby beets can be harvested at ping-pong ball size after about eight weeks. For pickling, let the beetroots grow for longer until they reach 5cm (2in) in diameter. Make repeat sowings directly into the ground if you have room, or sow into modules and plant out as young plants.

Good varieties include 'Detroit 2 Little Ball', which is deep red; 'Burpee's Golden', which is orange; and 'Barbabietola di Chioggia' which has pink roots with white rings. All young, tender beetroot leaves are excellent for adding to salads, but if you want them specifically for this purpose, sow some 'Bull's Blood' and you can pick from the same plants all summer.

TIP
The corky seeds of beetroot contain inhibitors which slow germination, so soak the seeds for half an hour before sowing.

A box of mini turnips

Make the most of your space by growing mini-turnips – you can eat the tops and the roots of these tasty vegetables.

Time to sow: Spring through to late summer.

Forget Baldric's tasteless old turnips – these baby roots are fast growing and full of flavour. Tender young baby turnips are a revelation to anyone used to tired old roots cut into chunks in a stew. The seeds germinate within days, which makes this a great crop for the first-time veg grower. They grow Incredibly fast, too – the first sowings are often ready to harvest in around six weeks.

Turnips grow well in large containers, pots or even old fruit boxes filled with soil or a soil-based compost, as long as they're thinned to about 7.5–10cm (3–4in) apart. If they grow too close together they will bolt and produce no roots.

As they're closely related to cabbages, the new young leaves can be harvested as a tasty leaf vegetable in March and April, when other crops are still getting under way.

Good varieties include 'Purple Top Milan', which has tasty flat-bottomed roots; and 'Snowball', which is perfectly white with a delicate flavour.

TIP
It is essential to keep them well-watered to produce a good crop, as turnips grow so rapidly.

Fruitful French beans

These beans offer a big harvest in a very small space. Varieties with attractively coloured pods are ideal for the potager or in containers.

Time to sow: Spring to mid summer.

Beans are easy to grow and extremely fruitful for the small-space gardener. Grow climbing types up a wigwam of canes or against a fence on a wooden or cane trellis. Dwarf varieties can be grown in pots and containers, or interplanted between slower-growing brassicas.

You can sow seeds outdoors from mid spring until mid-July. Sow them 5cm (2in) deep in the ground, or in pots indoors or in a cold frame in early spring. Dwarf varieties are best spaced 20cm (8in) apart in rows 20cm (8in) apart, and climbing types 15cm (6in) apart with 60cm (24in) between rows. Keep the plants well watered when in flower to help the pods set, and pick the crop regularly to ensure the plants produce more beans.

Good varieties include climbing 'Cosse Violette', which has purple pods; and 'Opera', which has good crops of green beans and is resistant to many bean diseases. 'Cobra' is another good choice for small gardens as it produces a heavy crop of tasty green beans over a long season. For really small spaces, try dwarf 'Sprite' for its green pods; and 'Purple Queen' for its tasty purple pods.

TIP
French beans are self-pollinating, so planting them close together produces better crops.

Carrots in beds

The flavour of home-grown, freshly pulled carrots is second to none.

Time to sow: Mid-spring through to late summer.

Growing your first batch of carrots every year is a delight. You can start the season off early by warming the soil with cloches. The secret to good carrots is a well-prepared, light, sandy soil that they can push their roots easily into without forking.

Dig and fork the bed through a couple of weeks before planting and rake the soil to a really fine texture. Hoe off or hand-pick out any weeds that appear, without disturbing the soil too much, then sow the small seeds thinly, following the spacings on the packet, and barely cover them with soil. This should reduce the amount of thinning you need to do later – which is good news because it's the smell of carrot thinnings that attracts carrot root fly, probably their worst pests. (See p186 for tips on dealing with these pests.)

Good varieties include 'Sweetheart', which is tasty and good for early crops; 'Flyaway', which has some resistance to carrot root fly; and 'Parmex', which is a ball-shaped carrot good for heavier soils.

TIP
Don't be tempted to sow outdoors too early in the season, as carrots need warm temperatures to germinate.

A wigwam of runner beans

Runner beans romp away once they've germinated, rapidly covering a wigwam, wall or trellis, or filling a container.

Time to sow: Late spring to early summer.

Sow individually in pots to a depth of about 5cm (2in) indoors or in the cold frame, or directly into the ground outside from the end of April/mid-May, allowing 15cm (6in) between plants. Transplant seedlings outside, into the positions where you want them to grow, when all risk of frost has passed.

Put wigwam frames or poles in place before you sow or plant outside, and train climbing varieties up their supports as they grow. This is particularly important if you are growing several plants, as beans grown in blocks tend to crop more heavily. Alternatively, train onto a trellis, arch or frame as an attractive and productive screen.

Keep runner beans well watered as they come into flower, and pick the beans when young for the best flavour, as this will help keep the crop coming.

Good varieties include 'Painted Lady', which has beautiful red and white flowers; and 'Red Rum', which has red flowers.

TIP
Remember that this is a warm-climate crop, originally from Mexico, so don't be tempted to plant it outside too early.

Plan your space

Making a simple plan of your garden will help you think through ideas and maximise your space.

Time to do: Autumn and winter.

It's worth taking a little time to think about the design and layout of your garden before you get planting, as it's easier to make changes on paper than on the ground. You don't need to be a garden designer to draw a plan, simply start by measuring out the space, then plot it out on a piece of graph paper.

Once you have your basic layout, mark on it any permanent features such as trees, ponds, paths, and so on. Also include the house wall and mark where the back door is, and which way is north. This is essential so you know which wall is south-facing and therefore sunny and warm – perfect for growing a grapevine or fan-trained peach tree. East- and north-facing walls are colder, shadier and better suited to growing a blackberry or hybrid berry.

Use this drawing as a template, make a few photocopies and play around with ideas, putting plants and beds in different places until you come up with something you like and that works for you and your space. Raised beds are ideal for small gardens as they contain your crops. You can also construct paths around them which means you can tend crops without compacting the soil. Chunky timber beds, like those pictured here, can also be a real design statement in their own right. (See p20 for how to construct raised beds.)

TIP

Try to include pots or a bed of herbs near to the kitchen door – if they're handy they'll get used all the time.

Making raised beds

Raised beds look good and allow you to crop intensively. They are easy to construct and really make the most of a small garden.

Time to do: Autumn and winter.

Treated with wood preservative, raised beds should last for years. They have many advantages, including the fact that you can grow plants closer together in raised beds than in open soil, and that you can walk around the beds.

Walking over the soil to sow, dig, weed or harvest will cause it to compact, which causes problems for many crops, but root ones in particular. Aim to make each bed about 90–120cm (3–4ft) wide so you can reach into the middle of the bed without stepping on the soil. Make sure the paths are wide enough to walk through easily, or even to push a wheelbarrow through.

You'll need some long pieces of wood (Tanalised, if possible, as they last longer) to make the sides of the bed. These can be anything from 15–30cm (6–12in) high. You'll also need some sturdy, pointed stakes to fix the side pieces to. Measure the beds as accurately as possible and dig out the paths to mound up the topsoil in the beds. Hammer the stakes into the ground with a sledgehammer inside the corners of each bed – and also halfway down if the beds are long – then nail the sides on. Spread out the soil evenly across the beds.

TIP
Keep your costs down by using recycled or salvaged wood, such as old railway sleepers or scaffolding boards.

Composting in a small space

Compost is a fantastic source of nutrients for your beds – and making your own is a good, free way to turn spent plants into something useful.

Time to do: All year round.

Garden compost is a valuable source of organic matter and nutrients, which are essential for growing good vegetables, especially if you're cropping more intensively in raised beds. You should add organic matter to most beds every year so the soil doesn't become depleted of nutrients. Although you can always buy manure, using your own garden compost is much more satisfying.

Make compost in specially designed compost bins, or construct them to fit your space using old pallets or floorboards. Whatever size your bin, it is important that you are able to turn the contents easily in order to aerate the heap and to get it to break down well.

You can put most things on the compost heap, such as grass clippings, debris from crops and other plants, but avoid adding any diseased plant material, as diseases can survive in a small-scale, relatively cool heap. Household kitchen waste, such as vegetable peelings and tea bags, can be thrown in too, but don't use cooked foods, as these tend to attract vermin. Compost prepared in summer should be ready for use after about three months, six in winter.

TIP
Compost bins come in all shapes and sizes. If you want to buy one, contact your local council first as they often sell them at a discount.

Making a seedbed

It really pays to take time to prepare your ground well before sowing seeds.

Time to do: Spring to autumn.

As a rule, the finer the seeds, the better worked the ground needs to be in order for them to germinate and grow well. Carrot seed, in particular, is very fine and needs a well-prepared bed, otherwise the seeds become buried under clods of earth and can't reach the light. Beans, however, have huge seeds that will thrust their way through all but the densest soil.

Every autumn, if you are between crops, dig some well-rotted manure into the bed. (Unless you are using the bed for root vegetables, in which case do not add manure as this will cause the roots to fork.) Break up any large clods of soil and compost as you fork over the bed thoroughly. Use a flat-headed rake – the heavier the better – to even out the soil in the bed and to remove any stones or twigs, or any weeds. Hand-pick out any persistent weeds.

Using the rake again, gradually work the soil into a fine 'tilth' – a lovely breadcrumb structure that is perfect for sowing seeds.

TIP
Always use a line to mark out seed rows if your beds are long – it is much easier to hoe between straight rows of plants later on.

Thinning and spacing between plants

Getting the spacing right between developing seedlings early on gives plants a great start.

Time to do: All year round.

However carefully you sow, seedlings will nearly always need thinning out to ensure each plant has the space it needs to grow to its full potential. The correct spacing for individual varieties will be found on the seed packet of whatever vegetable you are growing, so do use this as your guide.

It's easy to sow larger seeds, such as beans and peas, the right distance apart. Young plants sown in pots are also simple to space out correctly when transplanting outside. However, tiny seeds like carrots, radishes and parsnips always end up too close together and must be thinned out. If they aren't, plants tend to become stressed and fail, or they run quickly to flower and seed without producing a crop. Many root vegetables are especially prone to this if left too crowded.

Thin by carefully pulling all the unwanted seedlings from a row, leaving the strongest plants the correct distance apart. Always water the remaining seedlings after thinning out, to settle the soil.

TIP
Use your hand to hold down the soil around those seedlings you want to keep, as you pull the others out.

Buying ready-grown plants

If you haven't the time or space to bring on seedlings, using young vegetable plants is the perfect solution.

Time to do: Spring through to late summer.

It may cost more than seeds, but buying packs of young, healthy plants is handy if you're really short of the space and time needed to grow your own seeds. They are widely available from nurseries, garden centres, and mail-order or online from specialist seed companies or veg growers throughout the season. Young plants are an especially good option when it comes to plants that you only want a few of and that need warm, steady temperatures to germinate, such as tomatoes, chillies, cucumbers and peppers.

Young plants are also very handy for filling in a few gaps as the season wears on, and also for experimenting and trying something new. However, you don't get the range of varieties that are available from seed, and root crops such as beetroots and carrots shouldn't be bought this way as they don't like being transplanted.

TIP
Buy young plants of tomatoes and peppers in a few different varieties to see which ones you prefer.

Companion planting

Growing specific plants alongside vulnerable crops can help ward off pests without having to resort to chemical controls.

Time to plant: Spring and summer.

If you are keen to garden organically, particularly when it comes to food crops, you won't want to resort to chemicals and pesticides every time a pest comes along and attacks your plants. Non-chemical sprays and solutions are available, but one really natural way to deter pests in the first place is by 'companion planting'.

This method involves interspersing certain crops with specific plants that will provide a beneficial effect. This occurs in a variety of ways; from masking crops with a pungent aroma, visually hiding plants, or producing flowers that attract and feed benefical insects like hoverflies.

French marigolds and nasturtiums help to keep brassicas free from cabbage white butterflies, and they also help to deter whitefly from tomatoes. Florence fennel can help to attract beneficial predators such as lacewings into the garden, while many fragrant annual herbs, such as dill and chervil, are said to boost the growth and flavour of lettuces and other salad leaves. Perennial herbs such as rosemary and lavender ward off many pests, while leeks and onions planted in between rows of carrots deter carrot fly.

TIP
Choose plants such as French marigolds and nasturtiums for the dual purpose of adding colour to a small garden and protecting plants from pests.

Crop rotation made easy

Keep soil healthy by growing each type of crop in new places every year.

Time to do: Winter.

When the weather turns cold and the new seed catalogues are delivered for the year ahead, spend some time thinking about rotating your crops. The idea behind this is that you will get a better harvest if you don't plant the same type of vegetable in the same place every year. Changing their locations helps to combat pests and diseases within the soil and can even increase its fertility.

Divide your crops into four main groups: root crops, potato family (including tomatoes), brassicas (cabbage family), and legumes (peas and beans). Each group of crops is prone to similar problems, so moving them around helps to stop these diseases building up. Draw your veg plot and each bed in a notebook, and mark up where you will plant particular crops. Make sure that each of the four groups only grows in the same spot once every four years. This means rotating the crops from bed to bed or area to area every spring.

TIP
Plant potatoes in the weediest section, as their leafy growth will shade out the worst of the weeds.

Three sisters planting

Make the most of a small plot by growing three crops together in the same bed.

Time to sow: Spring

The ancient South American civilisations liked to make the most of their space by planting sweetcorn, squashes and beans together to maximise yields from a small space. These three plants also go particularly well together, because if planted in one large container or bed they help each other out through the season. The sweetcorn provides support for climbing beans, the beans provide nitrogen for the sweetcorn, and pumpkins cover the soil, suppressing weeds.

You can grow sweetcorn with either French or runner beans and with courgettes, squashes, marrows or pumpkins. Sow seeds indoors in pots during spring and plant out into their final growing positions in late spring or early summer.

TIP
It's best to provide an additional support of cane tripods for the beans, as they can take over the sweetcorn.

Super salads and leaves

Sow leafy vegetables that will crop all summer long.

Time to sow: Spring and summer.

Cut-and-come-again salad crops are great for picking regularly, a few leaves at a time. Spinach, mustards, many lettuces and chard are the best for frequent picking, producing tender new leaves every couple of days in summer. The brilliantly coloured stems and crinkled leaves of chard are great for adding to salads when young, and for steaming if they are left to mature.

Chard is very quick and easy to germinate and should be sown in spring for summer harvesting, and then again in mid-summer for a later crop.

Good varieties of chard include 'Bright Lights', which has stems of yellow, red, pink and white with large leaves; and 'Ruby Chard' or 'Rhubarb Chard', which has bright red stems and finer leaves.

TIP
Overwinter your summer sowing of chard under fleece for early pickings the following spring.

Improving your soil

Feed your soil, and your plants, and you'll be rewarded with abundant crops.

Time to do: Winter and spring.

A healthy, rich soil bursting with nutrients is bound to produce good crops. Adding plenty of organic matter while forking or digging over the beds in winter and spring will keep your soil fertile and moisture retentive for the coming season. (See p22 for tips on how to make your own compost.)

Dig well-rotted manure, garden compost or leaf mould into clay soils in winter, but leave sandy soils until spring, otherwise all the nutrients will be washed away in the winter rains. Always stack up manure and leaves to rot down thoroughly. Never use fresh manure as it's too strong and could kill your plants or, at the very least, take essential nitrogen from the soil as it rots down.

TIP
Adding manure to areas where you intend to grow root crops such as carrots and parsnips will produce forked roots if the soil is too rich.

Make compost with a wormery

In a small garden, a wormery offers a compact, space-saving way to make excellent compost and liquid fertiliser.

Time to do: All year.

A wormery allows you to make great compost and fertiliser simply by letting worms munch through all your household food scraps and peelings. These leftovers would attract vermin if put on the compost heap, but an enclosed wormery turns this waste into rich compost. In addition, the liquid drained off from the base of the wormery makes a brilliant liquid fertiliser when diluted with water.

You can buy purpose-built wormeries or make your own from an old compost bin, buying the worms from mail-order companies or using ones from an existing compost heap.

Worms will eat almost anything, but don't add too much food in one go – allow the worms to process the material a layer at a time. Don't add fish or meat waste, seeds or citrus peel, as the worms won't be able to digest these.

TIP
Site the wormery in a shady place to stop it getting too hot or drying out, and keep it covered to prevent flies becoming a problem.

Grow your own garlic

Growing garlic is easy and rewarding, producing a reliable crop.

Time to plant: Autumn and early winter.

Plant garlic from October to December, as it needs a period of cold to stimulate growth. Always buy your first planting of bulbs from a garden centre, nursery or mail-order catalogue, as supermarket garlic, which is for eating rather than planting, tends to grow poorly. You can then save some of your own bulbs for growing in subsequent years.

Plant cloves of garlic in a sunny spot. Make sure each clove has its own bit of the root base-plate attached, and sow it 7.5cm (3in) deep and 15cm (6in) apart. Leave them to do their thing, but occasionally push cloves back into the soil if birds have tugged them out of the ground. Harvest bulbs once the leaves start to yellow from early summer onwards, and dry them off in a cool, dry place before storing.

Good varieties include 'Thermidrome', which is specially selected for the UK climate; and 'Early Purple Wight', an early maturing garlic with purple bulbs.

TIP
If the plant produces a flower stem, nip it off to increase the size of the bulb.

Make the most of green manure

Save yourself work in spring by sowing empty beds with green manure.

Time to sow: Spring through to late summer.

Green manures are a clever way of improving the fertility of your soil while also stopping weeds getting a hold on empty beds. These fast-growing plants are simply dug back into the soil after a few weeks of growth, adding valuable nutrients, or put on the compost heap if left to grow all winter.

Many green manures will 'fix' nitrogen in the soil – particularly clover, winter field beans and lupins – while others, like buckwheat, help to break up heavy soil with their roots. Sow short-term green manures on light soils to improve their fertility and moisture-holding capacity. Cut the crop down or chop it up with a spade and leave to wilt before digging it into the soil a few days later.

Good options include buckwheat, which is a fast-growing, short-term spring and summer type. Mustard, winter tares, crimson clover and fenugreek can be sown from spring to late summer, while winter field beans can be sown from September to November and be left in the beds over winter until early spring, when they can be simply dug into the soil.

TIP
Winter field beans can also be harvested as an edible crop.

Chitting potatoes

Get potatoes off to an early start by chitting them before planting.

Time to do: Spring.

Chitting potatoes simply means encouraging them to sprout before they are planted, which gets them growing well before they go into the ground.

To do this, simply place the potatoes in an egg box or seed tray with the 'rose end' (the end with the most eyes) facing upwards. Keep them in a light place, though out of direct sunlight – for example in the spare room, kitchen, or by the shed window. After about six weeks the sprouts should be about 2.5cm (1in) long and the potatoes can be planted out into open ground or containers (see p64).

Good varieties include 'Cara', which is vigorous and crops well in a small space; 'Kestrel' is unpopular with slugs.

TIP
It is particularly beneficial to start early varieties off by chitting, as they have a shorter growing time than maincrop types.

Dig out perennial weeds

Get your crops off to a good start by clearing your beds of perennial weeds early in the year.

Time to do: Winter and spring.

Before you get sowing, you need to be sure that the area is clear of annual weeds, but also perennial weeds, otherwise these will suddenly appear again and again and be unwelcome competition for the growing crops.

These weeds will compete with crops for space, moisture and nutrients in the summer. They are difficult to dig out without disturbing the roots of your crops, so it's best to clear them out thoroughly when digging over the bare ground in winter and spring. It is also easier then because the soil tends to be moist and the roots can be lifted cleanly without breaking them.

Perennial weeds, such as docks and dandelions, have deep roots that can re-grow if any part is left in the ground, so you need to completely remove all the roots when weeding.

TIP
Do not compost the roots of perennial weeds – chop the leaves off and compost these, but burn or bin the root systems.

Grow fragrant fennel

Florence fennel grows swiftly and makes a good crop for a small space, as the bulbs, feathery leaves and seeds are all edible.

Time to sow: Late spring and early summer.

Florence fennel needs a sheltered, sunny site to grow well. It does need a little planning and attention, though, as It is prone to bolting if plants are grown too close together or lack regular watering.

Sow the seeds where they are to grow and cover them with fleece to improve germination, as they don't like temperatures to be too cool. You can remove this fleece in June or July, or whenever the weather settles into a long warm spell.

Thin the seedlings to 25–30cm (10–12in) apart and water to settle the soil. Keep them well watered in dry spells and harvest a few leaves whenever you need them. For bulbs, grow on until the bulbs reach tennis-ball size, which is when they're ready to harvest.

Good varieties include 'Zefa Fino', which is resistant to bolting; and 'Perfection', which is ideal for early sowing.

TIP
Allow a few plants to flower, as they'll attract beneficial insects. The seeds are also good in baking.

Unusual containers

Have fun growing crops in unusual pots.

Time to do: Spring and summer.

You don't have to stick to conventional pots to grow vegetables – anything will do, as long as it has adequate drainage holes and enough room for the crop to develop properly.

Old fruit crates, olive oil tins and metal troughs make fun containers that are large enough for crops such as baby beetroots and turnips, salad leaves, and all sorts of herbs. Or, as here, develop a kitchen theme with edible pot marigold flowers and salad leaves bursting out of an old bread bin, or a colander of radishes.

Make sure the container drains properly by drilling a few holes in the base, if there aren't any, and adding a layer of crocks over the bottom before putting in the compost. Some containers may be too well drained, such as crates and colanders, in which case you need to line them with perforated polythene in the same way as you would a hanging basket.

TIP
Use a multi-purpose compost rather than garden soil, which can contain weed seeds.

Herbs in pots

Many herbs thrive in window boxes and containers.

Time to do: Spring and summer.

A pot or two of mixed herbs placed just outside the kitchen door is always handy when you are cooking, and most herbs love the growing conditions of pots and containers.

Give herbs free-draining compost and a warm spot in the sunshine all summer long and they should thrive, especially annual herbs such as basil, parsley and summer savory. Many shrubby perennials, such as rosemary and thyme, are quite happy in pots for several years and can provide a winter garden with much-needed evergreen structure.

Rather than planting them singly, try grouping herbs together in a pot. Team perennials such as rosemary and marjoram together, then grow annuals such as basil and parsley in a separate pot, as they'll be easier to look after that way. Take cuttings of the herbs and bring them on, so when the plants start to outgrow their space, you can replace them with new, home-grown plants.

TIP
Plant any shrubs and perennial herbs that will be in the pots for several years in a soil-based compost, mixed with grit for improved drainage.

Salad in a trough

Plant an attractive container with lettuces and other salad leaves.

Time to sow: Spring and summer.

Salads are perfect crops for large pots and containers; they are quick and easy to grow and harvest. Salad leaves such as lettuces, chard and leafy mustards make trouble-free container plants. For one thing, they suffer less slug and snail damage than those grown in the ground, and they're easy to keep well watered, as long as the container is a good size.

Planters like this trough look great and the depth allows for plenty of compost, which will help the plants grow well. Place broken-up polystyrene chunks into the base of the trough, as this will improve drainage and reduce the amount of compost you need to fill it.

You could make it a complete salad in a bed by planting a few quick-growing crops such as beetroots and radishes alongside the lettuces.

TIP
For best results, use young plants grown in modules, although you could sow seeds directly into a planter of this size.

Tomatoes in containers

Growing tomatoes in pots is easy, if you keep them well watered and fed.

Time to plant: Spring and early summer.

There are hundreds of varieties of tomatoes available, and many have been developed specially for container culture. Although you can sow seeds early in the year, it's often simpler to buy ready-grown tomato plants from a nursery or garden centre – especially if you only need a few plants. You can plant these outdoors in late spring or early summer, once the risk of frost has passed.

Choose a large pot with plenty of room for the roots to grow, as tomatoes are vigorous, and place in a sunny, warm spot. Water regularly, probably daily in hot weather, adding a high-potash tomato feed every week in summer. Watering is the tricky thing to get right with tomatoes: too much and the flavour is spoiled, too little and the fruit becomes marked or the skins split. Sinking a finger into the compost to judge its moisture content will help. If in doubt, little and often is better than no water, followed by a good soaking.

Good varieties include 'Totem', a compact bush plant that's perfect for smaller containers; 'Gardeners' Delight', a cordon type; and 'Balconi Yellow', which has small yellow fruits.

TIP
Go for one of the bush types rather than a cordon variety, as they're far easier to grow and look much better in pots.

Blueberries in pots

Grow this 'super food' in pots for the best results.

Time to plant: Spring.

This fruit is ideally suited to growing in pots, as it needs a moist, acidic soil, which isn't found in many gardens.

Blueberries are a great, long-lasting and long-fruiting crop that should be planted in pots filled with ericaceous compost. They're reliably fruitful as long as they're watered with rainwater (which means setting up a water butt, if you don't already have one). The harvest is also considerably improved if you grow two or more blueberries that flower at the same time, as they will help pollinate one another.

Blueberries are attractive ornamental plants in their own right and often produce lovely autumn colours as the leaves fade. They are tough, hardy plants, but the spring blossom can be damaged by frost, so protect them with horticultural fleece if a cold snap is forecast. They also need regular pruning, as the fruits are produced on two- and three-year-old wood and you need to keep a steady supply of new branches coming. In winter, cut out any dead, diseased, or damaged stems, plus those that fruited the summer before.

Good varieties include 'Bluecrop', which is early fruiting; and 'Berkeley', a vigorous, mid-season cropper.

TIP
Protect the fruits from hungry birds by covering them with netting.

Crops in grow bags

The perfect disposable solution for growing crops in small spaces.

Time to sow: Spring and summer.

Grow bags are a brilliant disposable method of growing crops in gardens where space is limited. They can even be used on balconies or put by the back door to provide fresh herbs and salads at arm's reach.

Although most often used for growing tomatoes, you can also use them as a complete mini-veg plot by cutting out the whole of the top of the bag. Add a binding of parcel tape around the middle to stop the compost spilling out, and sow directly into the bag or plant up with young plants. Salads, such as rocket, lettuces, mustards, and round-rooted carrots can all be grown in this way, as well as annual herbs such as dill and coriander.

Once the grow bag is planted up, if you have space, sow some more seeds in modules a few weeks afterwards and grow them on alongside. These can then be used to replace any plants you harvest from the grow bag, or any that die.

TIP
Make sure you feed and water plants in grow bags regularly, as they will dry out quickly in summer.

Pots of potatoes

Potatoes will grow in almost any container and they make marvellous patio crops.

Time to plant: Spring until mid-summer.

Plant in spring for early new potatoes and again in mid-summer for a Christmas crop.

Potatoes will grow in pots, dustbins, specially bought potato barrels, and even black plastic bags, as long as the container is deep and has plenty of drainage holes. Place in a bright spot, put a layer of compost 10cm (4in) deep in the base of the container and place two or three chitted potatoes on top. Cover these with another 10cm (4in) layer of compost.

The wider the container, the more potatoes you can plant and the greater the harvest. A 30cm (12in) wide container will only hold one seed potato, but a 60cm (24in) one should hold about three to five.

Keep the containers well watered. Once the shoots reach 10–15cm (4–6in) above the compost, add another 10cm (4in) layer of compost, leaving the tips showing. Keep doing this until the shoots are within 5cm (2in) of the top of the container. Harvest the crop when the flowers appear, by tipping out the container and digging in with your hands to uncover the potatoes.

TIP
To grow a Christmas crop, it's best to move the container into a conservatory or greenhouse once the weather turns cold in autumn. Alternatively, move it into a sheltered spot near the house and cover the crop with fleece on frosty nights.

Mini runner beans

Dwarf varieties of runner bean make attractive container crops.

Time to sow: Late spring.

Pretty and productive runner beans grow well in a large container, and are happy to share the space with other crops or flowers.

Sow beans 5cm (2in) deep in modules or pots indoors and grow them on until the risk of frost has passed. In late May or early June, plant the seedlings up outdoors in a container filled with multi-purpose compost.

Space the plants about 10–15cm (4–6in) apart and provide a framework of twiggy sticks, canes or metal spirals for the beans to climb up. Underplant with trailing tomatoes, herbs or salads, or add a few flowers, such as climbing morning glory, for more colour. Water the container regularly, especially in hot weather.

Good varieties include dwarf 'Pickwick', which has red flowers and needs no support; or 'Hestia', which has red and white flowers but needs pea sticks to scramble up.

TIP
Feed occasionally with liquid fertiliser to give the plants a boost.

Grow mint in pots

Keep mint under control by growing it in a pot or container.

Time to plant: Spring and summer.

Mint comes in many different varieties and all the best ones grow brilliantly in pots.

There really is no other way to grow mint in a small garden than in a container. Most mints have incredibly invasive root systems, which means they can take over a small bed in no time at all. But despite their vigorous nature, they do grow well in large pots and containers, providing they have a sunny or slightly shaded spot and a rich, moisture-retentive compost. Ideally, mint should be planted on its own in a container, as it will rapidly take over a mixed pot of herbs.

For mint all winter, bring the pot indoors as temperatures drop, or you can root a cutting in late summer and grow it on in a pot on the windowsill.

Good forms of mint include Moroccan mint, which has a strong flavour and is the best variety for brewing as mint tea; and apple mint, which has furry leaves and a milder, delicate flavour that's good for cooking with peas. Eau de Cologne mint has bronze-green foliage and a strong, distinctive scent. It is ideal for a small garden, being hardy and responding to regular cropping with lots of new foliage.

TIP
Pick regularly or clip to keep the plants thick and bushy and to encourage new shoots.

Herbs in hanging baskets

Keep culinary herbs close at hand in a hanging basket outside the kitchen door.

Time to plant: Late spring.

Take advantage of a wall near the back door and plant up and hang a basket with a selection of your favourite cooking herbs.

Fast-growing leafy herbs make a pretty and practical hanging basket, and as long as they're within reach, you will even brave a spot of rain if you know you can quickly pick a handful. Any type of hanging basket will do: rustic woven ones are particularly fetching, and large wire one with coir liners, like this one here, are readily available at garden centres and nurseries.

Choose herbs that you use all the time; moss-curled parsley, marjoram, sage and thyme are always good for cooking, and chives, chervil and coriander are great for spiciing up salad leaves.

Water the basket regularly once it's planted, especially if it's on a sunny wall. Pick the leaves regularly, otherwise the basket will become overcrowded.

TIP
Pop in a couple of nasturtiums for a splash of edible colour.

Wild strawberries in wall pots

A container of dainty wild strawberries brightens up a dull corner.

Time to plant: Spring.

Alpine and wild strawberries are less demanding of rich soil and sunshine than their larger-fruited cousins. This makes them perfect container plants on their own or with other plants like the long-flowering, perennial daisy, *Erigeron*. They're also tougher and less prone to pests and diseases, and don't need netting to protect them from birds.

Wild strawberries flower and fruit beautifully all summer long, even in shady conditions. Grow them in pots and containers in a part-shaded spot and harvest the fruits to use as you would conventional strawberries.

Good varieties include 'Alexandria', which is juicy and enjoys a shady spot and moist conditions; and 'Fraises des Bois', a classic, small-fruited type.

TIP
Combine wild strawberries with conventional strawberries when making jam, for a fruitier taste.

Courgettes in containers

Grow a single courgette plant in a pot for masses of vibrant flowers, foliage and fruit.

Time to plant: Late spring.

Courgettes are bold, fast-growing plants that look brilliant in large containers. The bigger the pot, the better, as far as a courgette is concerned; with their dramatic leaves and big yellow flowers, they can make quite a statement in a small space. Large pots, a wooden crate lined with polythene and even an old wheelbarrow all make good containers, or you can build a mini-raised bed with willow hurdles or pieces of wood.

Sow seed indoors in spring, but don't plant outside until all danger of frost has passed. Harvest the courgettes regularly once it starts fruiting – they'll soon turn into marrows if you don't – and keep the plant well watered, as courgettes are thirsty growers.

Good varieties include compact-growing 'Venus', with dark green courgettes; and 'Gold Rush', with bright yellow fruits.

TIP
For a taste of Italy, stuff male flowers (the ones without the swelling courgette behind) with ricotta and herbs, dip in batter and deep-fry them.

Cabbages in crates

Grow big, leafy cabbages that are fit for kings. This old crate makes a good container to grow a couple of plants.

Time to sow: Summer-hearting cabbages in early spring, winter-hearting cabbages in late spring, spring cabbages in mid-summer.

With their big, bold leaves and dense hearts, cabbages are remarkably attractive container plants. Grow them as mini-vegetables to be harvested when they are the size of a large cricket ball, but leave a couple to grow on to maturity.

Any good-sized container will do, as long as there is enough room to space the plants far enough apart, otherwise they will bolt. Large fruit crates lined with perforated polythene and filled with compost are ideal for growing about four plants; two to be harvested young and two to grow on. Make sure you choose really attractive varieties for the boldest, architectural look.

Good varieties include 'Ruby Ball', a beautiful red variety; and 'Stonehead', a sturdy, green-leaved type.

TIP
Protect from pigeons with netting, if necessary, and remove any cabbage white caterpillars as you spot them.

Colourful cape gooseberries

Cape gooseberries make an unusual and exotic container crop.

Time to plant: Spring.

This container combines colourful, edible flowers with the dramatic papery lanterns of the ripening *Physalis* fruits. Cape gooseberry, or *Physalis edulis,* is an easy and unusual container crop. You won't get masses of fruits (and they are a rather acquired taste, being quite sharp), but they look beautiful and they make an interesting garnish, or you can mix them with other fruits to make jams and tarts.

Grow *Physalis* from seed, sowing indoors in spring, or buy young plants and start them off indoors, growing them on under cover until there is no longer a risk of frost. At the end of May, plant outdoors in a large pot or recycled container, along with edible nasturtiums or marigolds for a real show of colour. Position the pot in a sunny, sheltered spot and water and liquid-feed with tomato feed regularly once the lanterns appear. Harvest in late summer/early autumn once the husks have turned translucent and papery, and the golden-orange fruit shows through.

TIP
You can leave the ripe fruits on the plant until you need them.

Culinary container

A practical take on an elegant container.

Time to plant: Spring.

A clipped bay tree makes an attractive container look good all year round, but if you underplant with shrubby herbs and flowers you can make a front-door feature a useful one, too.

Fresh bay leaves have a stronger flavour in cooking than dried ones, which makes this a great plant to have to hand. Evergreen bay trees look great when clipped into formal shapes such as cones and balls, and they grow extremely well in containers of all sizes for many years. They can be planted alone for a very formal look, or underplanted with more herbs as well as a few flowers to brighten up the show in spring and summer.

Try underplanting with rosemary, sage and thyme for the perfect array of culinary herbs, or grow with bedding plants such as pansies, pelargoniums and even pots of bulbs for a seasonal splash of colour.

TIP
Trim formal bay trees back into shape in spring before they put on new growth.

Standard currant

Potted black-, red- and whitecurrants are fruitful and easy to manage in a small space.

Time to plant: Spring and early summer.

Currant bushes and trained standard plants are ideal for small gardens as they grow well in containers. One plant can produce a substantial quantity of fruit, providing it's kept well watered while the fruits are developing.

Grow them in a large container or pot in a fertile, rich soil with plenty of garden compost mixed in, and protect the fruit from birds with netting. Site the container in a sheltered position, away from cold winds in spring when the plant is flowering, as this can hinder the formation of fruit.

Good varieties include blackcurrant 'Ben Sarek', which is hardy and has a good flavour; redcurrant 'Red Lake', which produces masses of jewel-like fruits; and 'White Versailles', a classic white currant variety.

TIP
Currants prefer cooler conditions and are happy to grow in some shade.

Beetroots and carrots in containers

Grow root crops in containers for easy, trouble-free harvests.

Time to sow: Spring and early summer.

Producing long, straight carrots and blemish-free beetroots can be tricky in open ground. Both are favourites with slugs at the early stages of growth, and carrots can produce forked roots in stony soil.

Growing them in large containers overcomes these problems, as the young plants are well away from the attentions of slugs and a fine, free-draining compost should give you slender, fork-free carrots. Provided you water the plants well in the summer, you can also grow them closer together in the perfect conditions of a pot than you would in the soil, so even a small container can be surprisingly abundant.

Good varieties include beetroot 'Detroit 2 Little Ball', which is a bolt-resistant mini beet; and carrot 'Sugarsnax', which is sweet and tasty.

TIP
Get early crops by sowing a large pot of roots indoors in late winter to harvest as baby veg a few weeks later.

Plant thyme in gravel

This must-have herb for cooking takes up a tiny amount of space.

Time to plant: Spring and early summer.

Thymes need poor, well-drained soils to thrive and they love hot, dry sites. Plant them in a gravel path or in a sunny corner by a house wall and they'll be perfectly happy.

There are lots of different varieties, some tiny leaved and carpeting, others bushier and larger leaved, but all are good for cooking with. They also flower prolifically and, although the flowers are small, the plants become a mass of pink, mauve or white in the summer months. The flowers are also good for attracting pollinators such as bees into the garden.

Plants may need protection from winter wet, which can cause them to rot – covering them with a small cloche or a piece of glass raised up on bricks should do the trick.

Good choices include 'Minimus', which makes a tiny, dense carpet of leaves; lemon thyme which has a lovely flavour; and 'Doone Valley' with gold and green variegated leaves.

TIP
Trim off all the flowers after they've finished to keep the plants bushy and to encourage new growth.

Grow veg in borders

Get the most from your space by planting veg among your flowers.

Time to plant: Spring and early summer.

Pretty and productive vegetables can add a splash of foliage and fruit colour to flower beds and fill gaps throughout the season.

Many vegetables grow well when planted with ornamental plants. They need the same conditions as many border flowers, and with plenty of sunshine, water and good soil, they perform well and can be just as attractive.

Beetroot, coloured-leaved chards and the clustered rosettes of lettuces look lovely mixed in with annual flowers and bedding plants. For added drama, use sweetcorn, curly kale or wigwams of climbing beans to add height to a border.

Good varieties include beetroot 'Bull's Blood', which has rich, dark red leaves; and sweetcorn 'Minipop', which produces baby corn cobs perfect for stir-fries.

TIP
Keep sowing more pots of lettuces and salads so you can replace those you harvest and avoid creating gaps in your border.

Espalier apples and pears

Trained fruit trees take up little space and look beautiful.

Time to plant: Autumn to early spring.

Covering a wall or fence with an espalier-trained tree takes a little time but doesn't require a lot of space. Looking after an espalier apple or pear may sound difficult, but if you keep up with the winter shaping and pruning it's straightforward and hugely rewarding. You can train your own or buy ready-grown espaliers at specialist nurseries or good garden centres; they will crop more quickly but will cost more than an untrained tree.

To train a young tree, first fix wires horizontally to the fence or wall about 35–45cm (14–18in) apart. Plant an unfeathered maiden tree (that is, a very young one that hasn't branched yet) and remove the leading shoot above three good upper buds. The two lower buds should then each produce a shoot that goes along the wire, in opposite directions, in the summer. The following winter, train in these shoots along the wire and allow the new leading shoot, the third bud), to grow up. Carry on in this way until you have the required number of tiers – it will take a few years. In between this winter training, prune in mid-summer, shortening all side shoots to encourage flowering wood to develop at the base.

Good varieties include pear 'Doyenné du Comice', with a glorious flavour and large fruits; and apples 'Egremont Russet' and 'Lord Lambourne'.

TIP
Always plant at least 15cm (6in) away from the fence or wall to allow room for the trunk to grow.

Choosing small fruit trees

Get the right size tree for your garden.

Time to plant: Autumn to spring.

Small gardens need small trees to make the most of the space. There are hundreds of fruit tree varieties available, many in a range of sizes. Most tree fruits are grown on specially developed rootstocks that can restrict the growth of the tree, making it suitable for the smaller garden or for growing in containers.

Look out for varieties labelled as dwarf or very dwarf. For apples, these tend to be the rootstocks called M9, which eventually makes a tree about 2–3m (6–10ft) tall and is used for dwarf bush and cordon types of tree, and M26, which grows to a final height of 2.5–4m (8–12ft) tall and is used for espaliers.

Step-over varieties – those low-growing forms that are trained horizontally as edgings for beds (see p98) – are usually grown on the tiny M27 rootstock. Small pear trees, such as cordons, espaliers, and dwarf pyramid types, are nearly always grown on Quince C or Quince A rootstocks.

Good varieties include apple 'Sunset', which has a lovely flavour; and pear 'Conference', which is reliable and hardy.

TIP
If you only have room for one tree, try a 'family' apple tree – it has two or three varieties grafted on to one plant.

Grow a strawberry wall

Clothe a dull wall with delicate flowers and luscious fruit.

Time to plant: Spring.

The classic fruit of the summer makes a pretty and productive use of wall space. Strawberries will grow in just about any container, as long as they have a rich soil with plenty of organic matter or garden compost mixed in, and they don't get too hot and dry.

A sunny, sheltered wall is the perfect spot for tubs, wall containers and tiered troughs. As with any container, make sure you water regularly – every day in the heat of the summer and twice daily in high temperatures if they are in hanging baskets. On a weekly basis, add a high-potassium liquid fertiliser such as tomato feed.

After the last crop has been picked, remove all the old foliage and fruit stems and give the plants one last good feed. Leave them outside over winter and they will crop well the next year, but do replace strawberry plants with new young plants every four years.

Good varieties include 'Cambridge Favourite', which is reliable and delicious; and 'Flamenco', which produces fruit for a long period over the summer.

TIP
Protect developing and ripening fruits from birds with netting.

Make a rhubarb patch

The perfect crop for a forgotten corner.

Time to plant: Autumn, or spring and early summer.

Rhubarb really thrives in a sunny spot with a good soil, but it's very accommodating and will grow happily in a shady spot that you don't know what to do with. Once it has settled in, it will crop prolifically for years. Although rhubarb is not too fussy about site and soil, avoid planting it in waterlogged ground as the crown may rot.

Plant ready-grown plants in well-prepared ground, adding a generous helping of garden compost or organic matter. Allow the plant to grow for the first year and don't harvest the stems at all, as it needs to establish. Harvest only lightly in the second year and always leave a few leaves on the plant in following years to allow it to regenerate.

Good varieties include 'Champagne', with beautiful pink stems; 'Victoria', which is a strong grower; and 'Early Timperley' which is a variety awarded the AGM by the RHS.

TIP
Don't cut off the stems when harvesting – simply twist them off from the base.

Step-over apples

You can find room for this tiny tree in even the smallest garden.

Time to plant: Autumn to spring.

Step-over apple trees are ideal for small-space gardening. An apple tree is a must-have for any keen fruit grower, producing fruit reliably as well as adding blossom and colour to the garden.

Step-over varieties are trained to be low growing, only reaching about 45cm (18in) tall, and need to be pruned annually in winter to keep their shape. A framework of canes allows the branches to be tied in securely, and although they don't bear as much fruit as larger trees, they should still produce enough apples to make their care worthwhile. And they'll all be within easy reach for picking!

Plant the trees in a row at the front of a border to act as a miniature, fruitful hedge. Choose a sheltered spot, as the blossom can be damaged by late frosts, and prepare the ground well, adding lots of compost or organic matter to the planting hole.

Good varieties include 'Egremont Russet'; 'Fiesta'; 'Sunset'; and many others.

TIP
Aim to plant two or three varieties that flower at the same time, as this will improve pollination and ensure a good crop.

Blackberries on walls and wires

A true sight and taste of autumn.

Time to plant: Autumn to spring.

The attractive, apple-blossom flowers of a blackberry look lovely in summer and the fruit, synonymous with autumn, is perfect for pies and jams.

Blackberries are very fruitful and forgiving plants, as they will tolerate a shady spot and even a frost pocket – although a sunny, warm site will result in more fruit. They make an attractive flowering and fruiting plant for a wall or fence, and can be easily trained along wires, although the thornless varieties are much more pleasant to handle.

Allow plenty of space when planting, as the stems are very long, and position the horizontal wires about 30cm (12in) apart, training each stem up and down in a sort of weave as it grows.

Good varieties include 'Loch Ness', which is thornless and very prolific; and 'Oregon Thornless', another thornless variety which has attractive, deeply cut leaves.

TIP
Blackberries are very tolerant of wet, clay soils, but if you have a sandy, light soil you'll need to add plenty of organic matter to retain moisture.

Edible flowers

Use these flowers to add colour to the garden and your salads.

Time to sow: Spring and summer.

For centuries edible flowers have been used in salads and drinks to add colour and a hint of flavour. Annual plants such as pot marigolds (*Calendula*), nasturtium and borage are easy to grow and will often seed freely around the garden, providing you with flowers for years to come.

Sow the seeds in situ directly into the ground, or in individual modules or pots to plant out where you want them. Dot them around in gravel paths, or at the edges of beds to soften hard lines and add a 'cottage garden' feel to your design.

You can pick whole nasturtium blooms and calendula petals to use in salads, while borage flowers are traditional in Pimm's and lemonade. You can even freeze borage flowers in water in ice-cube trays, which you can add to drinks as a pretty garnish.

Good varieties include *Calendula* 'Orange King', with bright orange flowers; and nasturtium 'Alaska Mixed', with multi-coloured flowers and marbled leaves.

TIP
Deadhead spent blooms regularly to encourage the plants to keep flowering. Stop doing this towards the end of the summer, though, so you can collect seeds for next year.

A space for figs

Figs love a sunny wall and will grow well with very little root space.

Time to plant: Winter to spring.

As long as the space is big enough to dig a hole, a fig will grow well. In fact, they often do best if their roots are restricted, as otherwise they can become hugely bushy and leafy and bear little fruit.

Fig trees need plenty of sunshine and a really warm spot, as the fruits take all summer to develop. Keep the plant pruned back within the space each spring, and use wires and canes to train the branches flat against the wall or fence, tying them in with twine.

Remove all the larger figs that haven't fully developed each autumn, leaving the little embryo figs to grow and ripen the following summer.

Good varieties include 'Brown Turkey', which is very hardy and a prolific cropper; and 'White Marseilles', which has beautiful translucent flesh.

TIP
Plant in the ground, lining the sides of the hole with vertical paving slabs and filled to within 20cm (10in) of the top with broken bricks to restrict the roots.

Grow gooseberries in shady corners

If you have a cool, shady spot in your garden, try growing gooseberries.

Time to plant: Winter.

Although you'll probably get more fruit in a sunny spot, gooseberries are very tolerant and will produce excellent crops in a shady site. A couple of plants make good use of that difficult corner, but avoid planting where it is cold and frosty, and make sure it's sheltered from cold winds in spring when the plant is flowering, otherwise the crop could be ruined.

Allow plenty of room per plant, as each one can spread to 1.5m (5ft) wide, and prune in winter to stop it encroaching on paths and other plants. Feed it with a high-potash fertiliser in spring to encourage good fruiting.

If space is tight, gooseberries can be either bought or trained as half-standards or cordons, which can be squeezed into the tiniest of plots. With a bit of careful pruning of sideshoots and nipping off the top of the main shoot, you can get a good harvest from just one stem.

Good varieties include 'Pax', which is virtually thornless and shows good resistance to American gooseberry mildew; and 'Leveller', which has a lovely flavour.

TIP
So-called thornless varieties still have some spines but are much easier to pick than the painful thorny types.

Grapes on a sunny wall

Bring a touch of the Mediterranean to your garden with a juicy grapevine.

Time to plant: Early spring.

Train a grapevine on a sunny wall for a delicious, fruitful climber. They are easy and attractive to grow, with lots of vigour and plenty of lush leaves.

Pick your spot carefully, as grapevines can get quite big, although they're brilliant for brightening up a dull fence or pergola, especially in autumn when the leaves turn lovely orangey-red colours. They're tolerant of poorer soils, and as long as they have a warm, long autumn, can fruit remarkably well. Keep vines well watered in dry spells when they are fruiting, particularly if they are growing against a wall or fence and thus sheltered from rainfall.

Strict pruning is a must, otherwise the plant will be all foliage and no fruit. Aim to create an open framework of branches, and prune each shoot back to a few leaves after the flower truss. Make sure you protect the developing fruits from hungry birds by covering the vine with netting.

Good varieties include 'Boskoop Glory', with rich, dark grapes; and 'Maréchal Joffre', which produces good-sized fruits.

TIP
Thin some grapes from the bunches as they develop, to reduce the chance of mildew and encourage individual grapes to grow larger.

A pretty and productive patch

Small beds and lots of flowers can create a practical and attractive space.

Time to plant: Spring.

A potager is an ornamental vegetable garden where herbs, flowers and vegetables are grown in small beds as much for their good looks as their crops.

Herbs such as lavender and chives are traditional in these types of gardens, as are plenty of edible flowers and attractive foliage crops, such as ruby chard and lettuces. Flowering beans, golden-fruited courgettes and fruit bushes also look lovely, and you might even find a sunny spot for a globe artichoke plant, which produces huge, purple, thistle-like flowers.

Beds can be at ground level or raised; they look great with an edging of wooden planks, woven willow, bricks, or even low box hedges.

Good varieties include anything colourful, such as ruby chard, lettuce 'Pandero', and nasturtium 'Tom Thumb Mixed'.

TIP
Underplant taller plants such as fruit bushes with flowering herbs, including chives, coriander and chervil.

A shady corner for raspberries

A cool, shady corner is the perfect spot for raspberries.

Time to plant: Winter.

Just a handful of raspberry bushes will fruit steadily and reliably for about 12 years, if they're given the right start. They need a rich, fertile soil with plenty of organic matter dug in before planting, and a good mulch at the start of the growing season.

Grow a few plants in a shady corner by a fence or as a screen, spacing them about 35–45cm (14–18in) apart and spreading the roots out in the bottom of each planting hole. Set up a framework of posts and wires and tie in the stems as they grow. Protect the ripening fruit from birds with netting draped over the frame.

Raspberries are available as summer- or autumn-fruiting varieties, so if you're a big fan of the fruit, extend the cropping season by planting one of each.

Good varieties include 'Glen Ample', which is a summer-cropping type with masses of tasty fruits; and 'Autumn Bliss', which is a favourite late-fruiting variety.

TIP
Raspberries will cope with heavy shade providing the soil isn't poor and dry.

Pretty as a peach

Fan-train a peach tree for a feast of fruit and flowers.

Time to plant: Winter and early spring.

Peaches respond well to training and will produce a reasonable crop on a sunny, south-facing wall or fence if their stems are pruned and tied in to a fan-shaped framework. If you don't have suitable wall space, there are also several varieties available as dwarf versions. These can be grown in containers as small trees, but will produce full-sized peaches.

Peach trees are happy in a well-drained soil, but need mulching every spring to make sure the roots stay moist through the growing season. The plants are fully hardy, but their blossom needs protection from frost as they flower very early in spring. If a cold snap is forecast and the plant is in bud or flower, cover it with horticultural fleece. The other downside to this early flowering is that pollination is difficult without many insects around, so you may need to hand-pollinate trees.

A common problem for these fruit trees is peach leaf curl, which appears as red blisters on leaves that soon drop off. Infected plants should be sprayed with Bordeaux mixture and all affected leaves cleared away and disposed of carefully.

Good varieties include 'Peregrine', which produces lovely yellow-white fruit; and 'Rochester', which is tasty with yellow-fleshed fruits. 'Avalon Pride' is a new variety that is naturally resistant to peach leaf curl.

TIP
Protect developing fruit from hungry birds by covering with netting.

Timely protection

Be sure to get good crops by protecting your plants.

Time to do: Winter, spring and early summer, depending on the crop.

A little protection at the crucial time can make all the difference. Pests and late frosts can spoil your chances of a good harvest. Birds are particularly troublesome when it comes to fruit bushes, but a drape of fine-mesh netting pegged down or weighted with large stones will prevent them getting to the fruit before you. However, do bear in mind that wildlife and birds can get trapped in netting, so check it daily to ensure that no wildlife are harmed.

It's best to raise and support the netting with canes if you can, as this stops the foliage growing through and making the netting difficult to remove without damaging the plant.

Pigeons are especially fond of brassicas and can reduce them to a skeleton of leaf ribs virtually overnight. Again, a frame of canes covered with netting over the brassicas will help. Do this when they're planted out and leave in place until harvest time.

Fruit-tree blossom, especially on trained specimens, is very susceptible to late frosts, which can ruin your chances of a good crop. If frost is forecast, protect delicate blossom with fleece or polythene pinned over the plant, and again secure it with large stones at the base .

TIP
If you haven't got large stones, use tent pegs or U-shaped pieces of wire to secure netting into the ground.

Quick and tasty mini leaves

Cress and other microgreens take up little space and grow in no time at all.

Different cresses and microgreens add interest and flavour to your salads and sandwiches. Growing cress is something most of us have done as a child, usually sprouting the conventional 'mustard and cress' on trays of damp kitchen paper.

These days, chefs have embraced the idea of tender, tasty sprouting seeds, and now seed companies offer a range of other options to try. All are designed to be eaten as young seedlings, often 6–15 days after sowing, before their 'true leaves' appear. Many of these microgreens are highly nutritious. Broccoli cress is easy, colourful, and very good for you, while tiny coriander leaves, fennel shoots and radish shoots are fabulous additions to salads and make attractive garnishes for cooked dishes.

Seeds can be sown directly into beds or containers outdoors in late spring and summer and harvested when young, but for best results sow indoors all year round. Fill pots or seed trays with vermiculite, not compost, and scatter the seeds thinly on the surface. Place the pots on the kitchen windowsill or in the greenhouse to germinate.

TIP
Experiment with different flavours – onions, red cabbage and pea shoots are also very good.

Cropping to encourage more

The more you pick, the more plants produce.

Time to do: Throughout summer.

Harvesting regularly throughout the season keeps plants producing more leaves, beans, pods and fruits.

Crops that aren't harvested quickly often stop producing, as the plants form seeds and complete their life cycle. Regular picking of crops makes them produce more and keeps them small and flavoursome, rather than big, old and tasteless.

Beans and peas need to be picked as soon as they're large enough, even if you only get a handful, otherwise the pods soon swell and turn stringy as the seeds ripen inside. The plants then produce no more flowers and the pods stop forming.

Harvest courgettes every other day once the plant is in full swing, as a small courgette will swell into a huge marrow in no time at all. Salad leaves, such as cut-and-come-again varieties, rocket and chard, should be picked every week. Either cut them to 5cm (2in) above the ground or simply pluck off the outer leaves, leaving the centre to produce more.

TIP

Try to pick a little every day if you can, as crops develop swiftly during the summer months.

Watering wisely

Vegetables and fruit rely on a plentiful supply of water to keep them growing.

Time to do: Spring and summer, mainly.

Watering wisely and at the right time is essential for producing healthy, abundant crops. Plants are mostly made up of water and the soil acts as a reservoir for their roots.

Digging organic matter into the soil improves its water-holding capacity, and adding a thick layer of mulch to the soil surface helps to stop moisture evaporating. But when there's no rainfall, sometimes watering is essential. Try to save as much water as possible in water butts, and remove weeds regularly so they don't take up valuable moisture.

When you do need to water, give each plant or row of plants a thorough drink – don't just sprinkle the surface with water. Leaf and root crops need regular watering at all stages, whereas fruiting crops such as tomatoes and beans critically need watering when they're just planted, when they're in flower, and once the fruit begins to swell.

TIP
Water in the early evening to allow the soil and plants to soak up the moisture, and to reduce water loss by evaporation from the sun.

Fill in gaps

Keep beds productive by filling any spaces with pot-grown plants.

Time to plant: Early and mid-summer.

Growing a few spare plants in pots is always a good idea so that you can quickly replace any you lose to frosts or pests, or that fail or go past their best. It's also worth having a few extra plants to pop into gaps after root vegetables, garlic or lettuces have been harvested to keep a constant supply of produce coming all season.

Sow and grow on a few quick, leafy crop plants that can grow to a harvestable size in short periods of time. Good crops for filling seasonal gaps include salads, rocket and chard, plus some cabbages and pak choi, which can be harvested as baby vegetables.

Long-term crops, such as leeks and onions, can be easily started off and grown on in pots (but don't grow root vegetables this way, as they don't like to be moved and disturbed). Once a space is free and the seedlings are big enough, simply plant them out into vacated soil once the other crops have been harvested.

TIP
Fill gaps in pots and containers with edible flowers such as pot marigolds and herbs like parsley and coriander.

Good housekeeping

Help reduce the risk of pest and disease attack by making tidying up part of your weekly routine.

Time to do: All year round.

Routine inspections and a few key jobs take no time at all and can make the world of difference to your crops. Healthy, happy plants will produce a more bountiful harvest, so keep an eye open for disease and remove affected plants swiftly to stop infections spreading. Burn any infected plants or put them in the bin, not on the compost heap.

Try to do little things regularly, such as trimming off yellowing, fading leaves from brassicas to reduce the risk of disease and so that slugs and snails have fewer places to hide. A quick weeding session reduces competition for water and lets rain get to the soil and plants more easily.

Cushioning developing strawberries with straw lifts them off the soil and lessens the chance of them rotting. It also retains moisture in the soil, which is vital for the developing fruit. A thick mulch of scratchy straw also helps to keep slugs at bay.

TIP
Pick off pests such as cabbage white caterpillars and blackfly by hand before they get a hold.

Keep sowing lettuces

Sow lettuces little and often for salad all summer long.

Time to sow: Spring through to mid-summer.

Lettuces need very little space to grow quickly and crop consistently, but they do require plenty of water to grow well. The downside is that they tend to be ready all at once, and before you know it they're past their best. So, to keep a steady crop coming, it's best to sow a few seeds at a time and repeat-sow every couple of weeks through the summer months. This successional sowing is perfect for lettuce varieties where the whole head is harvested, rather than the cut-and-come-again types that should keep going all season long.

Sow a short row of seeds and thin to the correct spacing, or sow seeds into modules and plant out when they're large enough. Repeat-sow two or three weeks later, and again two or three weeks after that. Stop sowing in early August, as after that the plants may not have time to develop fully.

Good varieties include 'Little Gem Pearl', which is ideal for small spaces; 'Buttercrunch', which is a butterhead type; and 'Pandero', with deep red leaves.

TIP
Water the plants regularly, otherwise the leaves will become bitter.

Super-speedy crops

Keep your crops coming by sowing fast-maturing vegetables.

Time to sow: Spring and summer.

Quick-growing crops add variety to your meals in the summer months. A handful of radishes needs very little space and takes no time to grow – they can be ready to harvest in as little as five weeks. Keep sowing small amounts of fast-maturing vegetables, such as radishes and spring onions, to supplement the steady crops from beans, peas and cut-and-come-again lettuces. Such crops will fill any gaps in the vegetable patch; or you can even grow small crops in pots and window boxes.

Good varieties include radish 'Cherry Belle', which is round and bright red; and spring onion 'White Lisbon', a fast-maturing favourite.

TIP
Sow spring onions and lettuces in late summer for an early harvest the following spring.

Winter harvests

Home-grown crops are all the more special in the winter months.

Time to plant: Spring and summer.

Summer crops have to be harvested when they're ready, otherwise they go past their best, but the beauty of many winter crops is that they can be left to stand in the ground so that they can be harvested right the way through to spring.

Many favourite winter crops can stand until you need them, and then you can take as many – or as few – as you want, leaving the rest for another day. Leeks and cabbages can be treated like this, as well as Brussels sprouts, if you have room for them. The main problem is that if the ground becomes frozen, you may not be able to dig the crop up, so insulate it with a layer of straw held in place with fleece, weighted with stones.

Good varieties include leek 'Varna' and 'Musselburgh'; and cabbage 'January King' and 'Tundra'.

TIP
In mild areas, carrots can be left in the ground and covered with straw over winter.

Keep sowing herbs

Regular small sowings will keep you in fresh young herbs all summer long.

Time to sow: Spring and summer.

Growing a handful of culinary herbs in the garden, in pots or in window boxes, can transform a range of cooked dishes and salads with no effort at all. Just a sprig or two of freshly-picked herbs will add oodles of flavour to any recipe.

Many perennials, such as thyme and rosemary, can be cropped year after year, but some of the top culinary herbs are annuals and need to be sown fresh each year. These include coriander, basil, chervil and dill, but all these are also prone to producing flowers, setting seed and fading very quickly, well before the season has finished. So, ideally, you should make about three or four repeat sowings, about three weeks apart, to keep the fresh young leaves coming.

Sow seeds thinly on the surface of moist compost from spring onwards, cover with a thin layer of compost and put the pots on a warm windowsill. As the seedlings appear, re-pot the herbs into bigger pots and move them outside. Start picking leaves as soon as they are big enough for cropping.

TIP
Dill and coriander readily run to seed, but the seeds are actually very tasty, so save those from the fading plants while harvesting leaves from the new sowings.

Collect seeds for next season

Keep the seeds of your favourite varieties and they will give you many future sowings for free.

Time to do: Late summer and autumn.

Saving the seeds from a number of vegetables is easy and fun – and will save you money in the long run, too. It should also ensure good results; these plants have already adapted to your growing conditions, so they should perform well next year.

In late summer, leave a few of your favourite runner beans, peas, herbs and flowers unpicked. Instead, let them set seed and dry off in early autumn on the plant. Harvest the seeds when they are fully ripe and dry – usually turning a brown colour – by removing the whole seed head with secateurs and carefully placing it in a brown paper envelope or kitchen towel. Store seeds in labelled and dated envelopes in a cool, dry place until next spring.

Good plants to save seeds from include French and runner beans, peas, coriander, dill and pot marigolds.

TIP
Use the seeds the following spring, as they germinate best when fresh.

Parsnips for winter eating

Parsnips are a long-term crop with lots of flavour, so make them part of your crop rotation to harvest as you need them over winter.

Time to sow: Mid-spring.

Growing parsnips does take time, as they're sown in spring and ideally not harvested until after the first frosts, so they're as sweet as possible. However, you can dig them up earlier than that, especially if you prefer them as baby vegetables. Although parsnips take up room in the garden for a long period of time, they're a reliable and worthwhile crop to grow.

Sow the fine, papery seeds in drills on a still day, as they tend to blow away easily. Parsnips like finely-textured soil that they can send roots through easily, so good soil preparation is essential. Avoid recently manured or stony soil, as this makes the roots fork. Sow seeds thinly, around 2.5cm (1in) apart, in rows 30cm (1ft) apart, then thin the seedlings to 15cm (6in) apart once they appear. Do not transplant seedlings.

Good varieties include 'Avonresister', which is resistant to canker and good on poor soils; and 'Tender and True', a classic variety.

TIP
As parsnips are slow to germinate and grow, you can sow fast-maturing crops such as lettuces and radishes alongside to make the most of the space in spring.

Sow peas in loo-roll tubes

Economise with space and money by sowing pea and bean plants in toilet roll middles.

Time to sow: Spring.

The cardboard middles of toilet rolls make perfect biodegradable pots for deep-rooting legumes. Peas and beans are large and fast-growing plants and they need plenty of root room to develop properly. They also hate cold soil and can germinate very patchily if sown directly into the ground early in the season.

Start early peas off indoors in March, and save money and space by using toilet roll tubes instead of traditional plastic pots, which are wider and not as deep. Fill each tube with compost and plant one or two peas about 2.5cm (1in) deep.

Grow on until large enough to plant out, then harden off by putting the plants outside on warmer days, bringing them back in at night. Plant out without removing their tubes, as these will quickly rot away in the soil. Use twiggy sticks or netting to support the plants as they grow.

Good varieties include pea 'Feltham First', which is an early variety; and 'Sugar Snap', which produces sweet pods that can be left to form peas.

TIP
In mild areas, sow peas outdoors in autumn to overwinter for next season. Protect with cloches if the weather turns bitterly cold.

Grow a quick crop of pak choi

Leafy and nutritious pak choi takes hardly any time to grow. Pop a few plants into odd spaces as you harvest other crops.

Time to sow: Spring and summer.

Pak choi is a delicious baby vegetable that can be eaten whole, brasied or steamed, or the leaves tossed in stir-fries. Although an oriental leaf vegetable, it grows easily and so swiftly here that it's the perfect 'filler' crop. You can treat it as a cut-and-come-again and start harvesting baby leaves for salads after only about two weeks, or you can leave the plants to grow to full size within a couple of months. Don't let them grow for too long, though, or they will bolt and will become unappetising.

Choose F1 hybrids, as these are more resistant to bolting, and sow into modules in mid-spring, planting out good-sized plants once the frosts have passed. Harvest mature plants before the chilly days begin, as pak choi tends to bolt if the weather is too cold. Protect developing plants from pigeons with netting.

Good varieties include 'Joi Choi', which has some resistance to bolting; and 'Red Choi', which is nice in salads.

TIP
Water plentifully during the growing season for good crops.

Winter-cropping kale

Robust and hardy kale is excellent for winter picking – there are many attractive varieties that will provide a steady crop.

Time to sow: Late spring and early summer.

Kale is an easy and reliable crop for winter harvesting. It will grow in poorer soils than most other brassicas and doesn't tend to suffer from the same pest and disease problems, making it a perfect crop for inexperienced veg gardeners. It does need a fair bit of space, however, although just a few plants will give you regular pickings through the winter, because you only need to harvest a few leaves from each plant at a time.

Sow the seeds in modules or pots for planting out in mid- to late summer, once the plants are 10–15cm (4–6in) tall. Space them 45cm (18in) apart and earth up or firm the stems into the ground in autumn to reduce wind rock. Keep harvesting the younger leaves throughout the winter months, and compost older ones as these tend to be bitter.

Good varieties include 'Dwarf Green Curled', which is ideal for the smaller garden; and 'Redbor', which has attractive, curly, red leaves.

TIP
Stake plants in autumn if your garden is particularly windy.

Make your own comfrey feed

This organic liquid fertiliser is simple to make, and you can use it to feed all your crops.

Time to do: Late spring and summer.

Comfrey liquid feed is a marvellous all-round fertiliser that can be made cheaply and conveniently from home-grown plants. Although liquid feeds like this one don't last long in the soil, they do give plants a valuable boost in summer when growth is at its strongest.

Comfrey (*Symphytum* spp.) is a low-maintenance, ground-covering perennial which will romp its way through poor soils and can become rather invasive if not kept in check. This makes it perfect for hard cropping and putting on the compost heap, or using as a liquid feed.

To make liquid comfrey feed, gather handfuls of comfrey leaves and place them in a hessian or net bag, then steep in a water butt or large bucket of water for a couple of weeks. The resulting liquid is dark, oily and very smelly, but full of potassium. It can be diluted in a watering can to feed your crops at a rate of one part comfrey liquid to ten parts water.

TIP
If you don't have access to any comfrey, use nettles to make an equally beneficial feed.

Mulch to conserve moisture

Cut down on weeds and reduce the need for watering by mulching.

Time to do: Throughout the summer.

Fast-growing plants need plenty of water during warm weather to keep them growing and producing crops. Adding a thick layer of mulch after watering or rainfall helps to stop the water evaporating from the soil surface in the heat of the sun, and keeps the moisture close to the roots, where it is needed.

Simply add a thick 5cm (2in) layer of garden compost, well-rotted manure or bark chippings around the base of plants such as tomatoes, courgettes and beans on a regular basis. Lay it on the soil surface and do not dig it in.

TIP
Mulching helps to cut down on emerging weeds by smothering them and covering the seeds so they don't have enough light to germinate.

Swift spring onions

Get bumper crops from a small space by repeat-sowing spring onions.

Time to sow: Spring through to late summer.

Spring onions make a marvellous crop for the small-space gardener, as they can be planted close together and repeat-sown throughout the season. They are delicious in stir-fries and salads.

Seeds sown in late summer will overwinter to provide early pickings in spring, and even the thinnings can be snipped like chives and added to salads.

Spring onions are actually immature 'true' onions and need to be sown close together to prevent the bulbs developing. Sow them every couple of weeks from mid-February through to late August, in between slower-growing crops, for a continuous supply. Sow in drills 1cm (½in) deep in rows 10cm (4in) apart and water the drills before sowing if the soil is dry.

Good varieties include 'White Lisbon', which is tasty and quick growing; and 'Winter White Bunching', a reliable overwintering variety.

TIP
Water well in dry weather, especially before harvesting as it makes pulling the plants easier.

Cloches extend the seasons

A simple cloche can help to extend the growing season – placing one over the soil early in the year warms the ground ready for planting.

Time to use: Autumn to spring.

Many plants and seeds simply will not grow if the soil is too cold, so a cloche convinces the plants that spring is on its way. It also offers valuable protection from chilly winds and rain, which can rapidly kill fragile young plants.

Use it in February for sowing early broad beans and at the end of the season to prolong the summer warmth for crops such as lettuces. Cloches are also useful for drying off harvested crops, such as onions and shallots, before they're stored.

You can make your own cloche using clear plastic, polythene or glass, or buy one ready made. The simplest cloche can be created with polythene stretched over a series of wire hoops and pegged down – it's also easy to put up and pack up in the shed when you don't need it.

Good varieties for growing under cloches include broad bean 'Aquadulce Claudia' and lettuce 'Marvel of Four Seasons'.

TIP
Use the cloche hoops covered with netting as bird protection for brassicas in the summer months.

Grow basil indoors

Get a genuine taste of Italy at home by growing your own basil.

Time to sow: Spring.

Basil is an essential herb for Italian cooking, and is an easy and rewarding plant to grow indoors, where it loves the warm temperatures and sheltered conditions.

In March or April, sow a few seeds in pots in a warm spot in a greenhouse, conservatory or on a windowsill. The temperature needs to be at least 16°C (60°F), otherwise they won't germinate – and even then they germinate slowly. Once the seedlings are large enough, divide them up into individual pots or modules and grow them on. Pinch out the growing tips when they have a few leaves to encourage them to bush out.

Plant out into pots, window boxes or containers and harvest regularly to keep the plants producing more leaves. Before moving them outside, begin to acclimatise the young plants in June by putting them outdoors for a few hours at a time during the day, bringing them back in at night.

Good varieties include 'Sweet Genovese', with classic, large, fragrant green leaves; and 'Purple Ruffles', which has very dark, purple-black leaves and a delicious flavour.

TIP
Don't be tempted to move plants outside earlier than June, as basil is very tender.

Force mint in winter

You can have fresh mint at your fingertips even in winter. Plant just a few roots and you can have mint sauce whenever you want it.

Time to plant: Early autumn.

Mint is such a strong grower that it's easy and fun to force it for the winter months. Dig up a few roots from plants growing out in the garden in September and plant them in a container filled with multi-purpose compost. Lay the roots down lengthways on the soil surface and lightly cover with compost. Water and place in a greenhouse, conservatory or on a bright windowsill.

Keep the compost slightly damp, but be careful not to over water – check by pushing your finger into the compost. New shoots should start to appear within a couple of weeks. Pot them up and keep them indoors on a sunny windowsill. Cut leaves regularly throughout the winter and the plant will grow bushier and will keep going until spring.

TIP
Use an old olive oil tin or an attractive wine box lined with polythene as a container if you want to grow mint on the kitchen windowsill.

Grow winter lettuces

Keep the taste of summer coming over winter with home-grown lettuces.

Time to sow: Late summer.

Growing a handful of lettuces is great for those times when you feel like eating a winter salad but have none in the house. You can grow winter lettuces in grow bags or pots in a conservatory, greenhouse, or even in a large box on the kitchen windowsill.

Simply sow a few seeds in modules or pots in late summer and place in a bright spot until they germinate. Lettuces prefer cooler growing conditions, so make sure they are not in direct light. Thin out the weakest seedlings and leave the rest to grow on until they're large enough to transplant into pots or grow bags.

Lettuces can suffer from fungal diseases, so allow the air to get to them on warmer winter days by opening windows, vents or doors, or placing them outside for a couple of hours if they're in pots or a box.

Good varieties for growing indoors over winter include 'Winter Density' and 'Kwiek'.

TIP
Start off seeds in winter and early spring to provide very early spring lettuces.

Herbs under a bell cloche

Growing plants under cover doesn't just mean greenhouses and conservatories – mini-cloches also provide good, portable protection.

Time to sow: Early spring.

Bell cloches act as miniature greenhouses for smaller plants such as herbs. Many annual herbs are fast growing but need warmth to get them up and running. Bought bell cloches, or ones made from large plastic drinks bottles with the bottom cut off, give young herbs that little bit of extra protection in cold temperatures.

All sorts of herbs can be started off in pots on a windowsill or in a propagator early in the season, then planted out under cloches from mid- to late spring. Do it this way and they should provide you with leaves for snipping within a few weeks – much quicker than those sown directly outside. To settle herbs in well as you plant them out, place cloches over the vacant soil where you want plants to grow a few weeks before planting to warm up the ground.

Good options include parsley, chervil and summer savory.

TIP
Keep cropping parsley into winter by covering with a cloche in autumn.

Windowsill propagator

A windowsill propagator gets the vegetable garden off to an early start and helps to keep crops coming all summer.

Time to sow: Early spring.

A compact propagator is one of the best ways to make the most of your kitchen windowsill – a seed tray with a plastic cover will do perfectly well, but you can also buy heated types.

Bottom heat is useful for germinating many seeds, and a plastic cover with adjustable air vents allows the humidity to be controlled to provide perfect growing conditions.

Long-term crops, such as chillies, peppers and aubergines, can be started off early in the season and kept at a constant temperature indoors. Quick growers, such as salads and herbs, can be germinated rapidly throughout the season and then potted on swiftly to make room to sow more seeds.

Good options include tomatoes, aubergines, peppers, and many salads and herbs.

TIP
Use in summer to provide a quick crop of interesting mini leaves, such as broccoli sprouts.

Growing peppers and chillies in pots

Spice up your menu with freshly picked peppers and chillies.

Time to sow: Spring.

Sweet peppers and chillies make great plants for growing in the greenhouse, conservatory or even on a sunny windowsill. Their attractive and colourful fruits can be added to curries, salsas and stir-fry dishes.

Sweet peppers need more room than chillies and will grow to 60–75cm (24–30in) tall, depending on the variety. Some varieties of chilli reach only 15cm (6in) tall, while others grow to 60cm (24in).

Sow seeds in spring in a seed tray and place on a bright but not directly sunny windowsill, covered with a propagator or plastic bag until they germinate. Alternatively, buy ready-grown plug plants from the garden centre or nursery and pot on as necessary. The final pot size should be about 20–30cm (8–10in) in diameter, although it can be less for dwarf chillies.

Usually peppers and chillies branch well, but if they're a bit sparse looking, pinch out the tips when the plants are about 30cm (12in) tall to encourage bushiness. Mist the plants regularly when they're in flower using lukewarm water to encourage the formation of fruits.

Good varieties include peppers 'Redskin' and 'Topepo Rosso'; chillies 'Anaheim', and 'Pyramid'.

TIP
Chillies are more tolerant of fluctuating temperatures and haphazard watering than sweet peppers.

Crop your own cucumbers

Indoor cucumbers make interesting climbing plants in a conservatory or greenhouse.

Time to sow: Late spring.

Sow two seeds to each 7.5cm (3in) pot, placing the seeds in the pot on their edge and about 2.5cm (1in) deep. Remove the weaker seedling once they've germinated and grow the largest one until it has six or seven true leaves, then pinch out the tip to encourage the plant to branch.

Cucumber plants will fruit well in a conservatory or lean-to greenhouse in grow bags or pots. However, they do need a sturdy framework of canes or wires to scramble up. A humid atmosphere is also beneficial, so keep the compost moist and mist plants regularly with lukewarm water.

Cucumbers are also thirsty plants, needing lots of water when growth gets going and particularly on hot days when they are fruiting. Feed regularly with a general-purpose liquid feed, too.

Good varieties include 'Telegraph Improved' and 'Crystal Apple'. Many excellent new greenhouse varieties are available that offer good resistance to powdery mildew.

TIP
Remove the male flowers as they appear, as greenhouse cucumbers should not be pollinated or they become bitter. It's easy to tell them apart: female flowers have a small, swelling cucumber visible behind the flower, males don't. However, most new varieties are all female and rarely produce male flowers.

Aubergines indoors

Aubergines fruit best in long, hot summers and love the extra warmth of being grown indoors.

Time to sow: Early spring.

Steady, warm temperatures and good humidity are the secrets to success with aubergines, which makes them perfect crops for a warm conservatory or greenhouse.

Sow seeds in trays, 7.5cm (3in) pots or modules at 15–21°C (58–70°F) and place in a propagator, warm greenhouse or on a windowsill. Pot on from trays or modules once the seedlings have three leaves, then grow on for a few weeks, potting on as necessary. Plant out into final-sized pots, 30cm (12in) in diameter, or plant two or three into grow bags.

Aim for a steady temperature of 15–18°C (58–65°F) and keep the compost moist but not waterlogged, misting the plants regularly with lukewarm water. Stake the plants with canes as they grow and feed every other watering with a half-strength tomato fertiliser.

Good varieties include 'Ova', which has small white fruits; 'Bambino' with dark, 'baby' fruits; and 'Black Enorma' which produces a few huge, fat aubergines per plant.

TIP
Soak the seeds overnight in warm water to improve germination.

Sowing seeds

Get crops off to an early start by sowing seeds indoors.

Time to sow: Spring and early summer.

Make the most of your warm windowsills, spare room or conservatory to get some seeds sown before the final frosts are over.

Many seeds take several weeks to germinate and grow before they're large enough to plant out. Getting a few things started in a warm spot indoors means plants will be ready to go into the ground as soon as the weather turns milder.

Make the most of your space by sowing into cells or modules, as they don't take up as much room as pots, but do give the germinating seedlings enough root room to grow on for a few weeks before they need potting on or planting out.

Fill the modules with compost and tap firmly to settle it down. Try to sow only one or two seeds per module to save you thinning them out later. Start off salads and herbs such as parsley in this way, then when they're large enough to plant out, harden them off by putting them outside for a few hours at a time. Once they are acclimatised to the outdoors, plant them straight out into the garden under fleece or cloches.

Good options include lettuces, herbs, peppers, tomatoes and chillies.

TIP
Label each set of modules clearly, otherwise you could get very confused once they all start coming up.

Make your own mini-polytunnel

Don't waste money on expensive polytunnels – make your own.

Time to do: Early spring.

Start the season early with a home-made mini-polytunnel – it is ideal for bringing on early sowings of broad beans, peas and salads. You can easily move it around the garden to shelter new plantings, helping them get established and protecting them from cold and drying winds. It's just the thing to ripen off chillies and tomatoes, too, at the end of the season, as it's taller than most ready-made cloches.

An old, bendy tent frame makes the perfect support for a large sheet of polythene which can be pegged into the ground using the tent pegs. You can buy UV-resistant polythene for a few pounds, and have it cut to the desired length, at most garden centres. This will last longer than ordinary polythene sheeting, especially if you roll it up and store it in the shed when not in use. The tent frame stores easily too – simply dismantle the poles and pop them back in their bag for next time.

TIP
Keep the ends open in summer for
better ventilation.

Sprouting seeds

Grow your own tasty, healthy sprouting seeds for sandwiches or salads.

Time to do: All year round.

Sprouting seeds are super healthy and incredibly easy to produce. They take up no space at all and will grow whatever the weather is like outside. Try different types of seeds for different flavours and crunchiness, and add them to salads, sandwiches and stir-fries. You can buy specialist seed-sprouting trays, or you can just use a jam jar.

To sprout seeds in a jar, soak the seeds in water overnight (sometimes longer for mung beans), then rinse them a couple of times. Use a sieve for larger beans or put a piece of muslin secured with an elastic band over the top of the jam jar for small seeds such as alfalfa. Rinse the beans and seeds daily like this and keep them at a room temperature of 20°C (68°F). The sprouts and shoots are usually ready to harvest within about a week.

Good options include alfalfa, which has a fresh pea taste; and mung beans – the 'bean sprouts' used in Chinese cookery.

TIP
Some seeds, such as alfalfa, need to be kept in the light, while others such as mung beans, produce longer shoots if kept in the dark.

Grow your own lemons

Turn your patio into a Mediterranean terrace with a fragrant lemon tree.

When to plant: Spring and summer.

A lemon tree makes a lovely feature plant on the patio in summer, with its fabulously scented flowers, glossy aromatic foliage and ripening fruits.

These citrus plants are equally lovely in winter, too. Lemons and oranges should be moved into a greenhouse, conservatory or bright porch in autumn to protect them from frost. This warmth should also bring out the scent from the lemon flowers and foliage.

Lemons take little effort to grow in pots, as long as they're carefully watered and fed every month during the growing season. Citrus plants dislike lime, so when watering use rain water or filtered water rather than straight from the tap.

Good varieties include 'Four Seasons', which has large fruits and can make a sizeable tree; and 'Eureka', which is smaller but also reliable and fruitful.

TIP
Take care not to over water or under water lemons – check the compost with your finger and aim to keep it evenly moist.

Common pests – vine weevils

These little white larvae can make a real meal of your crops in pots.

Time to take action: Spring and summer.

Vine weevil larvae can be a problem if you grow lots of crops in pots; as they will live in the compost and eat the roots of plants and seedlings.

Vine weevils love to lay their eggs in containers of compost, and their larvae can destroy crops from the bottom up, eating away the entire root system of a plant. So check the compost for these distinctive white, legless grubs with a brown head.

Luckily these pests are very easy to control with biological nematodes, which can be watered on to the compost and last for several weeks. The treatment is expensive, but if you grow a lot of things in pots then a couple of applications during the summer months are well worthwhile.

The adult weevils – dull-black beetles – are relatively easy to spot as they're very slow moving and have distinctive bent or 'elbowed' antennae. They are mainly nocturnal and tend to hide in dark corners during the day, so keep an eye open for them at dusk.

TIP
A good way to catch the adults is to place toilet roll tubes or small pots filled with straw in pots and containers. Check the traps regularly and destroy any adults you find.

Common pests – whitefly

These small but destructive pests often appear on plants in large numbers in greenhouses and conservatories.

Time to take action: Spring and summer.

Whitefly suck the sap of plants such as tomatoes and cucumbers, often hiding on the underside of their foliage. They also attack young plants and seedlings, as well as houseplants.

These pests are difficult to eradicate once they become established, so check plants regularly and take action as soon as you spot any. They weaken plants and disfigure them with spots on the leaves, sticky honeydew, and sooty moulds.

In the greenhouse, a biological control such as the tiny parasitic wasp *Encarsia formosa* can be used – a good garden centre will have details of suppliers, or serach online. Alternatively, hang yellow sticky cards above plants in the greenhouse to trap them. In the house, use a small hand-held vacuum cleaner to suck them off the plants.

Sprays are available for whitefly control. Follow the directions carefully as these only kill whitefly and not their eggs. Regular spraying is required to kill newly emerged adults before they lay more eggs.

TIP
The yellow traps catch whitefly that fly up when disturbed. So brush the foliage of infected plants with your hands to get the pests moving.

Common pests – blackfly

A familiar sight to many, these clusters of black aphids can quickly cover a plant.

Time to take action: Early and mid-summer.

Broad beans and nasturtiums are often affected by blackfly. Dense clusters of tiny pests can spread rapidly, sucking the sap and weakening the plant enough to ruin the crop.

The good thing about blackfly is that they are very easy to spot. They appear in late spring and early summer, clustering on the soft tips of plants and on the developing bean pods of broad beans in particular. They're also common on many flowering plants, especially nasturtiums, and once they get a hold they're hard to get rid of completely.

Act early by pinching off the growing shoots of broad beans and nasturtiums, and squirt off small clusters with a jet of water or squash them by hand. If the problem is severe, organic sprays are also available.

TIP
Encourage natural predators into your garden, such as blue tits and ladybirds, by putting up bird and bug boxes.

Common pests – slugs and snails

The bane of every gardener's life...

Time to take action: Spring.

Slugs and snails love seedlings and tender young crops. Slugs decimate ground-level crops and emerging seedlings, while snails are also energetic climbers and will readily find their way into containers and pots.

It is when plants are small and succulent that they are particularly vulnerable to slugs and snails. Once plants have reached a good size and are growing strongly and fruiting consistently, they can usually survive all but the worst slug attacks.

The best ways to deal with these unwelcome visitors are to use organically approved slug pellets little and often around crops, or to go on regular slug and snail hunts at dusk, disposing of them by whatever method you prefer. Some gardeners chop them up, drown them, or transport them some distance away. Beer traps are another popular choice, but do remember to empty them regularly. Copper rings or tape around pot rims are also very effective, giving snails a tiny electric shock when they pass over them.

TIP
Use barriers such as grit, broken egg shells or other manufactured slug gels and barriers to prevent slugs and snails getting to your crops.

Common pests – carrot root fly

Protect your carrot crop from these menaces in the summer months.

Time to take action: Early summer.

Simple protection methods will keep your carrots free of carrot root fly. These pests lay their eggs in the soil near carrots, and the larvae munch their way through the core of carrots from early summer until autumn, destroying the crop.

Sowing seeds thinly helps prevent the problem, as the adult flies are attracted to the smell of carrots when you're thinning the crop. They're also low flying, so a simple barrier only 30cm (12in) high all the way around the carrot bed will protect them. Use canes and fleece or polythene secured with string or wire. Alternatively, cover the entire crop with a thin-gauge fleece or a densely woven mesh so the light can still get to the crop.

If you have space, grow onions or chives around your carrots, as the smell from these will help disguise that of the carrots and should deter the flies.

Good carrot varieties include 'Flyaway' and 'Sytan' – both of which appear to be less attractive to the pest.

TIP
Delay harvesting carrots until autumn to avoid attracting the adult flies.

Storing potatoes in sacks

Make your harvest last all winter.

Time to do: Late summer.

Dig up maincrop potatoes in late summer and you can store them to keep you going over winter. Most maincrop potato varieties store exceptionally well over several months simply kept in brown paper or hessian sacks.

Dry the harvested potatoes off by laying them out on newspaper in a shed, conservatory, greenhouse, or even the spare room. Cover them with more paper or an old curtain and allow them to dry off for a week or two before carefully placing them in the sacks. Make sure they are not bruised or damaged, and that there are no signs of rot or slug holes. Put any damaged ones aside and eat them quickly.

Store the sacks of potatoes in a cool, but not cold, place – a garage is ideal – and check regularly for any signs of rot. Keep them in the dark to prevent them from sprouting.

Early and second-early potatoes cannot be stored in this way. They keep well in the fridge or a cool shed or a garage, but only for about a week. So if you grow these, harvest them only as and when you need them.

TIP
Store different varieties in different sacks so you can do a taste and storage test.

Apples for keeps

With a little careful preparation, you can be eating apples long after harvest time.

Time to do: Autumn.

You can store many varieties of cooking and eating apples through the winter. Even a small apple tree can produce a surprising quantity of fruit.

Apples are prolific fruiters, especially 'Bramley's Seedling' and other cooking varieties. It's worth storing some to see you through the winter months. Only store the best-quality fruit – eat those with any bruises or blemishes straight away.

Check the fruit carefully first, then wrap in newspaper or put them in plastic bags pierced with several holes and store in boxes or trays in a cool, dark place, such as a garage.

Unwrap and check the fruit regularly for any signs of rot or softness. Remove and use any that show signs of deteriorating.

TIP
Store wrapped apples in boxes, crates or even filing trays.

Making fruit jams

Preserve bumper crops of home-grown fruit by making jam with them.

Time to do: Summer and autumn.

Jams are a brilliant way to store huge quantities of fruit.

Soft fruits always seem to ripen at the same time – strawberries, currants, plums and gooseberries – all delicious and all needing to be used swiftly before they spoil. Making jam is a wonderful way to preserve the fruit and enjoy its flavour all year round. It takes a little effort, but is very rewarding and you can have fun trying different combinations.

Large amounts of fruit also disappear into tiny jars, which make far more sense for storing, and you and your friends and family don't get fed up with seasonal gluts of soft fruit.

All you need to make jam is an equal quantity of fruit and preserving sugar and plenty of sterilised jars. Boil the fruit and a little water for 10 minutes, then add the sugar and boil for another 10–15 minutes. Drop a little jam onto a saucer cooled in the fridge; if the surface of the jam wrinkles when prodded, it is ready, if not, boil for another 5 minutes. Put the jam into jars, seal, and they can be stored in a dark cupboard for up to a year.

TIP
Try making apple jams first to get your hand in, as these often set very readily.

Make a string of chillies

Brighten up your food and kitchen with this cheery way of storing chillies.

Time to do: Autumn.

Store chillies in the traditional way by threading them on a string. This is how they do it in Spain and Mexico – freshly picked chillies are hung up to dry to strengthen their flavour and boost their heat.

Strings of chillies look great in the kitchen and make lovely Christmas presents too. Harvest chillies in late summer and autumn by cutting them from the plant, leaving a long stalk on each fruit. Use red or green string for a seasonal look, and tie the chillies on in small bunches of four or five in several clusters up the string. Add a parcel label with the variety name on it, if you like, and leave a long piece of string at the top to make a loop for hanging it up.

TIP
Chillies contain a strong irritant, so wash your hands thoroughly after handling them and don't rub your eyes.

Storing onions and garlic

Plaited into strings, onions and garlic keep for months and are easy and space-saving to store.

Time to do: Late summer.

Garlic and onions are must-haves for cooking, and if stored in plaited strings they're always on hand for use.

Onions and garlic must be really ripe and dry to store well, especially if you make them into strings like this. If one bulb rots, it will infect the bulbs next to it and the whole string could be ruined – so keep checking the bulbs to make sure none are deteriorating.

Once you've harvested your onions, lay them on the ground under cloches or put them in the greenhouse or conservatory to dry off thoroughly. The skins should become papery and dry to the touch. Then simply bunch together the onions to form an attractive string or weave the strong, rope-like tops together to make a plait.

TIP
Onions also store well in old nylon tights, but these don't look as good hanging in the kitchen!

Easy irrigation tips

Set up a watering system early in the season to save you time and worry later on.

Time to do: Late spring and summer.

Watering in summer can be time consuming, but there are ways in which you can simplify the process; either by using automatic or timed systems, or by linking up drippers into pots or containers that can water several plants with one turn of the tap.

Beat the hosepipe bans by setting up as many water butts as you have room for by the house, greenhouse and shed, so they're handy for your herbs and vegetables. For the best water uptake, attach seep hoses or lengths of ordinary garden hose punctured with a nail every 30cm (12in) to water beds and borders in the evening.

Check out the internet or local garden centres for handy reservoir watering systems for use outdoors or in the greenhouse – they're great for water-sensitive tomatoes. You can also set up dripper systems on a timer, if you have a lot of pots and containers and are often away. A huge variety of irrigation systems are available, and many can be attached to water butts as well as taps.

TIP
Shade newly planted seedlings and young plants with newspaper or netting placed over a bamboo frame on hot days, to stop them losing too much moisture.

Planting in containers

Container gardening is perfect if you're short on space – it is practical and fun on a balcony or in a tiny garden.

Time to plant: Spring and summer.

Most crops will grow well in containers, providing the pot is large enough to allow the plants' roots to develop fully. As a general rule, the larger the pot, the better the plants will grow, and this is especially true of long-term plants such as fruit bushes and trees. Short-term crops can be grown in smaller pots and boxes, though, as they don't have time to develop extensive root systems.

When transplanting pot- or module-grown plants, always re-plant at the same level. Place some broken up polystyrene or old pots in the bottom for drainage, then part-fill the new pot with compost. Make a hole in the compost for the plant, then settle it in gently, trying not to damage any fragile roots. Top up with compost to the level at which it was planted before, and firm the plant in with your hands. Don't bury the stem of the plant beneath the compost, as this could cause rot to set in. Don't leave the roots above the compost either, as the plant could dry out.

TIP
Water newly potted plants well to settle the compost around their roots.

Winter-prune apple trees

Prune apples and pears in winter to get the best shape.

Time to do: Winter.

The winter months offer the ideal opportunity to get apple and pear trees looking good and growing well.

After leaf fall in autumn, the trees are dormant and pruning cuts have time to heal well before the trees burst back into life in spring. Also, without leaves you can see the shape of the tree more clearly, which makes it easier to decide which branches to prune.

Always remove any dead, diseased or badly damaged branches first, and then try to create an open shape, removing any weak or spindly growth to encourage other branches to thicken up.

Keep a mixture of older stems and new growth, because if you cut back too hard you could have little or no fruit the following year. Cut branches back to the junction with another large branch, or even the trunk, rather than just trimming off lots of spindly branches, to ensure a good fruit crop the next year.

TIP
Cut back the tallest leading shoot every year to keep the tree at the size you want.

Summer pruning

Peaches, nectarines, plums and damsons all perform better when pruned in summer.

Time to do: Spring and summer.

Spring and summer is the best, if not only recommended, time for pruning plums and damsons, as they are prone to silver leaf disease, which can infect them if they're pruned in winter. As with other fruit trees, start with any damaged, diseased or dead branches first, and then only prune further if absolutely necessary.

In spring, on peaches and nectarines, simply rub off with your finger and thumb any shoots that are growing in the wrong direction – towards the wall or fence on fan-trained trees, for example. Then, in summer, pinch out the new shoots you don't need to create a framework of stems about six leaves long.

After cropping, these pinched-out shoots can be trimmed back to three leaves to stimulate fruiting buds to form next season.

TIP
For fan-trained trees, train in new stems every year to fill any gaps in the framework.

Recycling ideas

Be kind to your purse and the environment and grow seedlings in containers made from household waste.

Time to do: All year round.

With a little ingenuity and time you can re-use a number of things that would otherwise end up in the bin.

Washed-out margarine tubs, yogurt cartons and milk containers make marvellous pots for growing seedlings, if you punch a few drainage holes through the bottom.

Cardboard cartons and toilet roll tubes are brilliant for growing deep-rooted beans or sweet peas. There's no need to remove them when planting, either, as they'll quickly rot away in the soil. Egg boxes can be used like small peat pots for growing lettuces and herbs, and will also rot in the ground. Re-use white plastic bottles or margarine tubs by cutting them into pieces to make labels, and save foil trays, free CDs and tin foil to make bird scarers by tying them together with string.

TIP
Small yogurt-drink pots make excellent cane toppers to protect your eyes and stop protective netting becoming holed.

Plant bare-root trees and shrubs

Winter brings a slowdown for plants and gardeners, making it the perfect time to plant bare-rooted trees and shrubs.

Time to plant: Winter.

Bare-root trees and shrubs are a cheap way of buying plants, and are available for sale from nurseries and mail-order companies in winter. This is the best time to plant these trees and shrubs, as they settle in and establish more successfully if they're planted after leaf fall, when they're dormant.

Take time to prepare the planting site in advance, and ideally plant your trees or shrubs as soon after you receive them as possible in order to get them off to a good start.

Dig out a large enough hole to accommodate the root system, and fork over the base, mixing in some garden compost and bonemeal. Arrange the plant in the hole, spreading the roots out. Use a cane to check that you are planting it at the correct level. The soil mark on the stem should be level with the soil surface. Backfill the hole with a mix of topsoil, garden compost and bonemeal, firming down with your feet as you go. Finish off by giving the plant a thorough watering and make sure it is well watered for the next few months.

TIP

If staking your tree, position the stake alongside the tree before filling the planting hole with soil again.

Index

Picture credits

BBC Books and *Gardeners' World Magazine* would like to thank the following for providing photographs. While every effort has been made to trace and acknowledge all photographers, we should like to apologise should there be any errors or omissions.

Peter Anderson p17; Mark Bolton p67 (design: Bob Purnell), p89 (design: Bob Purnell); Torie Chugg p57 (design: Paul Williams), p103; Sarah Cuttle p9, p37, p79 (design: Helen Riches), p85, p109, p131, p153; Paul Debois p81 (design: Cinean McTernan), p157, p175, p183, p191 (Abigail Dodd); Melanie Eclare p119; *Gardeners' World Magazine* p177; Michelle Garrett p163; Stephen Hamilton p11, p27, p71, p94, p107, p115, p121, p151, p159, p201; Sarah Heneghan p133; Neil Hepworth p15; Caroline Hughes p31, p135, p149, p171; Jason Ingram p19 (designer: Nick Williams–Ellis, Hampton Court Flower Show 2008), p21, p25, p35, p45, p52 (design: Jekka McVicar/Lisa Buckland), p54 (design: Jekka McVicar/Lisa Buckland), p61, p69 (design: GW Live, Garden of three R's), p75 (design: GW Live, The Good Life with Bradstone), p77 (From Life to Life Garden for George, Chelsea Flower Show), p87, p99, p111 (design: Summer Solstice Garden, Chelsea Flower Show 2008: del Buono Gazerwitz, Spencer Fung Architects), p127 (Toby Buckland), p129, p139, p143, p195, p197; Lynn Keddie p63; Gavin Kingcome p161; Noel Murphy p59, p113; David Murray p83; Tim Sandall p23, p29, p33, p39, p41, p47, p49, p65, p73, p91, p93, p97, p101, p105, p123, p125, p137, p141, p145, p155, p165, p167, p169, p179, p181, p199, p203, p205, p207, p209; Nick Smith p43, p117, p147, p173, p185, p187, p189, p193; William Shaw p13, p51

Save over 25%
when you subscribe

Subscribe to *Gardeners' World* Magazine for just £15.75 and receive the best gardening advice and fresh ideas delivered to your door every month.

How to order

To subscribe call **0844 848 9707** and quote GW10108 Lines open Monday to Friday 8am-8pm and Saturday 9am-1pm

Visit **www.subscribeonline.co.uk/gardenersworld** and enter the code GW10108